one word.

Yolanda Toney

BookLeaf Publishing

India | USA | UK

Presentation by *BookLeaf Publishing*

Web: www.bookleafpub.com

E-mail: info@bookleafpub.com

ISBN: 9789357446068

First edition 2022

DEDICATION

I dedicate *one word.* to every individual who has been silenced because the voice of the enemy has tried to speak louder than the voice of God.

ACKNOWLEDGEMENT

I acknowledge Abba, my Heavenly Father; my former English instructors; Terrance Toney, my older maternal brother; Marvin Jones, my biological father; and Horace Drake, my stepfather.

PREFACE

Though poetry lends itself to the visual beauty of words written that become the soothing sounds of spoken word from someone who speaks eloquently well, the author however provides an explorative quest where she becomes acquainted with herself while becoming the spiritual being whom the Creator called and destined her to be. Therefore, she writes with intention to feed your soul through grammatical intensity, cultural awareness, and spiritual enlightenment. Thus, please allow the author to surround you with the light that causes darkness to wander alone.

Name

Noun.
A person, a place, a thing, or an idea.
Proper noun.
A specific person, a specific place, a specific thing, or a specific idea.
Abstract noun.
An untouchable person, an irreplaceable place, an immovable thing, or an invisible idea.
Gender.
Male or female.
Masculine.
Boy, man, or gentleman.
Feminine.
Girl, woman, or lady.
Yolanda.
Rochelle.
Toney.
My name is...
I am female.

Yolanda

You overthink like a never-ending data analysis.
Overthinking limits ambition not depressive
anxiety.
Let anxiousness never doubt ability.
Abort nonsense during adventures.
Neglect dreary aggression.
Daydream always.
Accelerate!

Rochelle

Renew or channel holistic energy like lurking eagles.
Oblige chatter hindering everlasting life labeled eternal.
Choose happiness, enjoyment, laughter, liveliness, exuberance.
Have enchanted, long lasting engagements.
Exchange love languages endlessly.
Limit lust exclusively.
Learn effortlessly.
Execute!

Toney

Teach others new elevations yearly.
Oppose nor eliminate yourself.
Never envy youth.
Enjoy yesterday.
Yearn!

Questions

Inquire.
Inquisitive.
Interrogate.
Interrogative.
Investigate.
Investigative.
If you inquire, you become inquisitive.
If you are inquisitive, you begin to interrogate.
If you interrogate, you become interrogative.
If you are interrogative, you begin to ask.
Ask.
Asked.
Challenge.
Challenged.
Examine.
Examined.
If you ask, you will receive answers to the
questions asked.
If you asked the right questions, you could
challenge the validity of the answers given.
If you challenge the trusted answers, you have
challenged the mind to think.
If you challenged the mindset, you would begin
to examine the identity of the responder.
If you examine the recipient, you have examined
the mind, body, and soul.

If you examined the totality of the individual,
you would soon earn a level of trust.
Questions are only asked to inquire, to
interrogate, and to investigate the truth.

Who

Who am I?

I am whom the Creator called and destined me
to be.

Who are my parents?

I am the daughter of a chocolate melanin queen,
a light-complexioned king, and a bonus king of
Native-American descent.

Who are my siblings?

I am the only sister of a maternal brother who
was born several years before me but perished
during his less-than-a-month infancy.

I am also the only sister of two living and one
deceased paternal brothers who are all much
older than me with adult children of their own.

Who have I been?

I have been an honor student, student council
president, senior class favorite, college graduate,
and graduate student.

Who will I become?

I will become a best-selling author, a doctor of
education, an entrepreneur, a wife, and a mother.

Who am I destined to be?

I am destined to be the answers to the questions
for others that God placed inside of me.

Who will I always be?

I will always be a believer, a daughter, a niece, a
cousin, a friend, an educator, and a
world-changer.
I am the whom I am supposed to be.

What

What makes me amazing?
Does being amazing make me beautiful?
What makes me beautiful?
Does being beautiful make me confident?
What makes me confident?
Does being confident make me delicate?
What makes me delicate?
Does being delicate make me eloquent?
What makes me eloquent?
Does being eloquent make me fierce?
What makes me fierce?
Does being fierce make me generous?
What makes me generous?
Does being generous make me happy?
What makes me happy?
Does being happy make me intense?
What makes me intense?
Does being intense make me jumpy?
What makes me jumpy?
Does being jumpy make me klutzy?
What makes me klutzy?
Does being klutzy make me lenient?
What makes me lenient?
Does being lenient make me merciful?
What makes me merciful?
Does being merciful make me nimble?

What makes me nimble?
Does being nimble make me oblique?
What makes me oblique?
Does being oblique make me practical?
What makes me practical?
Does being practical make me quick-witted?
What makes me quick-witted?
Does being quick-witted make me righteous?
What makes me righteous?
Does being righteous make me solemn?
What makes me solemn?
Does being solemn make me thoughtful?
What makes me thoughtful?
Does being thoughtful make me unique?
What makes me unique?
Does being unique make me versatile?
What makes me versatile?
Does being versatile make me wily?
What makes me wily?
Does being wily make me xenacious?
What makes me xenacious?
Does being xenacious make me yon?
What makes me yon?
Does being yon make me zippy?
What makes me zippy?
Does being zippy make me amazing?

When

Second.
Minute.
Hour.
Day.
Week.
Month.
Give me a second.
Wait a minute.
Be ready in an hour.
Every day counts.
Every week ends.
Every month begins.
Each day counts because it has seconds.
Each week ends because minutes have passed.
Each month begins because it has new hours.

Yesterday.
Today.
Tomorrow.
Past.
Present.
Future.
Never.
Always.
Sometimes.
Yesterday was.

Today is.
Tomorrow will be.
Yesterday was the past.
Today is the present.
Tomorrow will be the future.
Yesterday was never today.
Today is always the future.
Tomorrow will sometimes be yesterday.

Where

Anywhere.
Everywhere.
Nowhere.
Somewhere.
Anywhere I want to be.
Everywhere I am supposed to be.
Nowhere I have to be.
Somewhere I ought to be.
I do not want to be anywhere.
I am not supposed to be everywhere.
I do not have to be nowhere.
I ought not be somewhere.
Anywhere with anyone doing anything is not
what I want.
Everywhere with everyone doing everything is
not how I am supposed to be.
Nowhere with no one doing nothing is not
whom I have to be.
Somewhere is not why I ought to be.

Why

Because I am whom I am.
Because I beseech whom I beseech.
Because I carry whom I carry.
Because I desert whom I desert.
Because I entertain whom I entertain.
Because I forgive whom I forgive.
Because I gauge whom I gauge.
Because I honor whom I honor.
Because I invite whom I invite.
Because I juxtapose whom I juxtapose.
Because I know whom I know.
Because I lead whom I lead.
Because I meet whom I meet.
Because I notify whom I notify.
Because I obey whom I obey.
Because I praise whom I praise.
Because I quiz whom I quiz.
Because I satisfy whom I satisfy.
Because I teach whom I teach.
Because I utilize whom I utilize.
Because I value whom I value.
Because I watch whom I watch.
Because I xerocopy whom I xerocopy.
Because I yowl whom I yowl.
Because I zero-in whom I zero-in.

How

I love that the first question "who" and the last
question "how" have the same letters!
I love that the "who" is always unknown and the
"how" is always unpredictable!
I love that the "who" is always mysterious and
the "how" is always momentous!
I love that the "who" is always a person and the
"how" is always a process!
I love that the "who" is always a well of wisdom
and the "how" is always a wealth of knowledge!
I love that God is the "who" is always the same
to me and the "how" is always His same
precedence over me!
I love that God is the "who" is always
omniscient and the "how" is always His
omnipotence!
I love that God is the "who" is always
miraculous and the "how" is always His
majesty!
I love that God is the "who" is always a
promise-keeper and the "how" is always His
performance!
I love that God is the "who" is always willing
and the "how" is always His wonders!
God is who and how, regardless if the letters are
rearranged.

Fanboys

Can boys be fans?
For boys can be fans.
And boys can be fans.
Nor boys can be fans.
But boys can be fans.
Or boys can be fans.
Yet boys can be fans.
So boys can be fans.
Coordinating conjunctions want to know.

Fanboys can be for you.
And fanboys can be against you.
Fanboys can never be by themselves nor beside
themselves.
But fanboys can be found between other words.
Fanboys can be compound or complex.
Yet fanboys can be complicated.
Fanboys can always be used, so they can be seen
often.
Subordinating conjunctions will never know.

For

A conjunction that is relatively small
Because it obviously only has three letters.
A conjunction that is phonetically sound
Because each letter is pronounced loud and
clear.
A conjunction that is easily forgotten
Because sometimes writers do not know when to
use it.
A conjunction that is rarely used
Because most people do not understand its
intent.
A conjunction that is prepositionally placed
Because it offers a provisional annotation.
A conjunction that is biblically noted
Because Jeremiah 29:11 and John 3:16
contextualizes it best.

And

A three-letter word
That is supposed to join words, phrases, and clauses
When the opportunity presents itself.
A three-letter word
That comes with an unexpected attitude
From a melanin queen
Who is trying to understand someone else's point.
A three-letter word
That might create an argument
Based upon the tone of the speaker
Who does not quite care about the other person's feelings.
A three-letter word
That could possibly cause confusion
From a statement
Where the intention is unknown.
A three-letter word
That can easily be avoided
If it is not used as an initial response
When someone is reacting to an interactive conversation.
And...there you have it!

Nor

Neither you nor I agree.
Neither you nor I behold.
Neither you nor I contend.
Neither you nor I doubt.
Neither you nor I engage.
Neither you nor I forget.
Neither you nor I galvanize.
Neither you nor I harass.
Neither you nor I interject.
Neither you nor I judge.
Neither you nor I kindle.
Neither you nor I lack.
Neither you nor I motion.
Neither you nor I nag.
Neither you nor I objectify.
Neither you nor I provoke.
Neither you nor I qualify.
Neither you nor I resist.
Neither you nor I swear.
Neither you nor I transcend.
Neither you nor I unlearn.
Neither you nor I vitalize.
Neither you nor I win.
Neither you nor I xeriscape.
Neither you nor I yammer.
Neither you nor I zap.

But

I am anxious about few things,
But I am not anxious about everything.
I am benevolent about offering,
But I am not benevolent about stealing.
I am crazy about love,
But I am not crazy about hate.
I am decisive about most things,
But I am not decisive about my faith.
I am eager about my future,
But I am not eager about death.
I am fond about my family and friends,
But I am not fond about the enemy.
I am gentle about my spirit,
But I am not gentle about my flesh.
I am happy about my life,
But I am not happy about my consequences.
I am integral about my career,
But I am not integral about dishonesty.
I am jovial about respecting others,
But I am not jovial about rudeness.
I am knowledgeable about education,
But I am not knowledgeable about marriage.
I am learned about grace,
But I am not learned about long-suffering.
I am mild about spice,
But I am not mild about peace.

I am nice about helping people,
But I am not nice about ridicule.
I am open about my struggle,
But I am not open about romance.
I am pretentious about my character,
But I am not pretentious about
misrepresentation.
I am quiet about my personal business,
But I am not quiet about entrepreneurship.
I am radical about my beliefs,
But I am not radical about politics.
I am solid about friendships,
But I am not solid about disloyalty.
I am truthful about God,
But I am not truthful about idols.
I am universal about music,
But I am not universal about racism.
I am vain about my purpose,
But I am not vain about potential.
I am wasteless about food,
But I am not wasteless about hunger.
I am xenial about clients,
But I am not xenial about opportunists.
I am yearnful about companionship,
But I am not yearnful about deception.
I am zealous about abundance,
But I am not zealous about the lack thereof.

Or

Either I accept myself or not.
Either I believe myself or not.
Either I check myself or not.
Either I date myself or not.
Either I enjoy myself or not.
Either I find myself or not.
Either I groom myself or not.
Either I honor myself or not.
Either I improve myself or not.
Either I justify myself or not.
Either I know myself or not.
Either I love myself or not.
Either I motivate myself or not.
Either I nourish myself or not.
Either I occupy myself or not.
Either I protect myself or not.
Either I question myself or not.
Either I reward myself or not.
Either I secure myself or not.
Either I treat myself or not.
Either I uplift myself or not.
Either I value myself or not.
Either I work myself or not.
Either I x-ray myself or not.
Either I yoke myself or not.
Either I zest myself or not.

Yet

The anticipation that something will avail...
The belief that something will begin...
The choice that something will change...
The decision that something will divulge...
The evolution that something will erupt...
The frustration that something will fail...
The gesture that something will give...
The hope that something will heal...
The inkling that something will ignite...
The junction that something will join....
The known that something will ken...
The link that something will loosen...
The motivation that something will move...
The niche that something will navigate...
The option that something will open...
The pause that something will prevail...
The quarrel that something will quicken...
The result that something will reveal...
The stop that something will start...
The truth that something will transpire...
The understanding that something will unite...
The validation that something will vex...
The wish that something will wade...
The x-factor that something will Xerox...
The yield that something will yclept...
The zone that something will zoom...

So

The two-letter word
That usually causes the most unexpected
disciplinary action
From the queen of her tribe
Who does not tolerate disrespect.
The two-letter word
That usually caused us melanin children
To get a forceful backhand slap
Across the smack of our lips.
The two-letter word
That usually offers a gesture of unconcern
When someone simply does not care
What another person is saying.
The two-letter word
That usually begins most conversations
When a sistah is about to spill the tea to another
sistah
Who is anxious about what the other sistah is
about to say.
The two-letter word
That usually starts with a sigh of hesitation
When someone is unclear and/or unsure of/about
something
Because the something was unexpected.
The two-letter word
That usually introduces itself in a song

Where it tells people to go "all the way to
Mexico."
So...

Men

Amen!
Has anyone ever wondered why "Amen" is
pronounced as *a man*?
Has anyone ever wondered why "Amen" is not
spelled as aman?
Has anyone ever wondered why "Amen" is not
genderfluid where there is also Awomen?
Has anyone ever realized that "Amen" has the
prefix "a" which means against?
Has anyone ever realized that "Amen" could
possibly mean against men?
Has anyone ever realized that "Amen" uses men
in a plural context rather than singular?
Has anyone ever noticed that "Amen" solidifies
the truth that is spoken after every prayer?
Has anyone ever noticed that "Amen" could
possibly represent the Trinity, even though They
are three in one?
Has anyone ever noticed that "Amen" is a
complete sentence all by itself?
Has anyone ever known "Amen" to be the most
repetitious word in our spiritual lives?
Has anyone ever known "Amen" to be the
sanctity and the sanity of men in our lives?
Has anyone ever known "Amen" to be the
blessing that we need to bless others?

Well...I have wondered why, realized that, noticed that, and known Amen to be the healing response in my life.
Since I am the church, let me say, "Amen!"

Terrance

A man whom I have never known
Because he was born several years before me
But he died during his infancy.
A man whom I have always long to know
Because he would have been my maternal
brother
But had a different father.
A man whom I will never know
Because he did not live long enough to meet me
But he watches over me.
A man whom I wish I could meet
Because he was born to the same woman as me
But he did not get a chance to know her for long.
A man whom I wish I could know
Because he carried the same legacy as me
But he perished before he could create a lineage
of his own.
A man whom I desire to meet one day
Because he is walking the streets of gold
But he never lived to acquaint himself with
family.
A man whom I desire to see later in life
Because he will be introduced in the spirit to my
children
But he will only be spiritually present.
A man whom I desire to find in heaven

Because he has been living his best eternal life
But he thankfully never lived in the streets.

Marvin

A man whom I wish I knew more about
Because I am often asked about my heritage.
A man whom I only knew for fifteen years
Because he died a few weeks after my fifteenth
birthday.
A man whom I deeply love
Because he planted his seed for me to grow.
A man whom I am much alike
Because our college majors are very similar.
A man whom I found humorous
Because his wit was unmatched.
A man whom I respected
Because he never disowned or neglected me.
A man whom I will always honor
Because he was a man of integrity.

A man whom I continue to make proud
Because his legacy will leave an imprint on
Earth.

Horace

A man whom I knew in my single digits until I
was thirty-two

Because my mom met him when I was nine.

A man whom I knew as my stepfather
Because my father was still alive and well.
A man whom I loved dearly
Because he admired, honored, and respected my
mom unconditionally.
A man whom I loved and still love to this day
Because he never emotionally, mentally, or
physically abused or mistreated me.
A man whom I treasured and still do
Because he was and will forever be a hidden
jewel.
A man whom I represented while on Earth
Because he was a gift to many but golden to me.
A man whom I will never regret
Because he taught me the importance and power
of prayer.
A man whom I will never forget
Because he laid breathless on his living room
floor one Tuesday afternoon…
Until I found him and called 911.

Brother

A male sibling
Who can either be maternal, paternal, or both.
A male species
Who can either be biological, spiritual, or both.
A male relative
Who can either be a close cousin, friend, , or
both.
A male person
Who should be treated like a human being and
nothing else.
A male citizen
Who should be treated with dignity, honor, and
respect.
A male companion
Who should be treated like a king.
A male confidant
Who is honest, stable, and trustworthy.
A male encounter
Who is cordial, pleasant, and reserved.
A male employee

Who is diligent, persistent, and resilient.
My maternal male sibling
Whom I never knew as a species, relative,
person, citizen, companion, confidant,
encounter, or employee.
He was the late Terrance Alonzo Toney.

Father

A male parent
Who plants a seed

For the seed to grow.
A male parent
Who prepares the way
For the mother to give birth.
A male parent
Who sets a positive environment
For the child to receive love.
A male parent
Who provides for the household
For the family to be stable.
A male parent
Who gives his all
For everyone to thrive and survive.
A male parent
Who creates a legacy
For his offspring to maintain.
A male parent

Who becomes proud of his children
For every award and accomplishment.
My father
Who did not live long

For me to show him that I graduated.

Stepfather

A bonus male parent
Who does not get the service
He deserves.
A bonus male parent
Who does not get the trust
He deserves.
A bonus male parent
Who does not get the esteem
He deserves.
A bonus male parent
Who does not get the platform
He deserves.
A bonus male parent
Who does not get the favor
He deserves.
A bonus male parent
Who does not get the awareness
He deserves.
A bonus male parent
Who does not get the time
He deserves.
A bonus male parent

Who does not get the honor
He deserves.
A bonus male parent

Who does not get the encouragement
He deserves.
A bonus male parent
Who does not get the respect
He deserves.
My stepfather…
Let's just say…
    Society needs to take the prefix *step-*
            away.